My Legs Are Long and Strong

by Joyce Markovics

Consultants:
Christopher Kuhar, PhD
Executive Director
Cleveland Metroparks Zoo
Cleveland, Ohio

Kimberly Brenneman, PhD
National Institute for Early Education Research
Rutgers University
New Brunswick, New Jersey

BEARPORT PUBLISHING

New York, New York

Credits

Cover, © iStockphoto/Thinkstock; 4–5, © John Snelling/Getty Images; 6–7, © Guy Edwards/naturepl.com; 8–9, © A & J Visage/Alamy; 10–11, © Gallo Images/Alamy; 12–13, © GFC Collection/Alamy; 14–15, © iStockphoto/Thinkstock; 16–17, © Gallo Images/Alamy; 18–19, © Otto Plantema/Foto Natura/Minden Pictures/Corbis; 20–21, © Otto Plantema/Foto Natura/Minden Pictures/Corbis; 22, © Fred Bruemmer/Getty Images; 23, © Aaron Amat/Shutterstock; 24, © iStockphoto/Thinkstock.

Publisher: Kenn Goin
Senior Editor: Joyce Tavolacci
Creative Director: Spencer Brinker
Design: Debrah Kaiser
Photo Researcher: Michael Win

Library of Congress Cataloging-in-Publication Data

Markovics, Joyce L.
   My legs are long and strong / by Joyce Markovics ; consultant: Christopher Kuhar, PhD, Executive Director, Cleveland Metroparks Zoo, Cleveland, Ohio.
      pages cm. — (Zoo clues)
   Includes bibliographical references and index.
   ISBN-13: 978-1-62724-108-3 (library binding)
   ISBN-10: 1-62724-108-6 (library binding)
   1. Ostriches—Juvenile literature. I. Title.
   QL696.S9M37 2014
   598.5'24—dc23
                                    2013035387

For more information, write to Bearport Publishing Company, Inc., 45 West 21st Street, Suite 3B, New York, New York 10010. Printed in the United States of America.

10 9 8 7 6 5 4 3 2 1

Contents

What Am I?

Look at my neck.

4

It is long
and thin.

5

I have feathers
on my body.

6

They are black and white.

I have two
large wings,
but I cannot fly.

8

My eyes are
huge and round.

I have two large
toes on each foot.

My beak is pink
and pointy.

14

My legs are long
and strong.

17

What am I?

Let's find out!

I am an ostrich!

Animal Facts

Ostriches are the largest birds on Earth. Like all birds, they lay eggs. They also have feathers, wings, and a beak. Unlike most birds, ostriches cannot fly.

More Ostrich Facts

Food:	Plants and sometimes insects and lizards
Size:	7 to 9 feet (2 to 3 m) tall
Weight:	220 to 300 pounds (100 to 136 kg)
Life Span:	30 to 40 years
Cool Fact:	Ostriches can run up to 43 miles per hour (69 kph)!

Adult Ostrich Size

Where Do I Live?

Ostriches live in Africa. They live on grassy plains or in deserts.

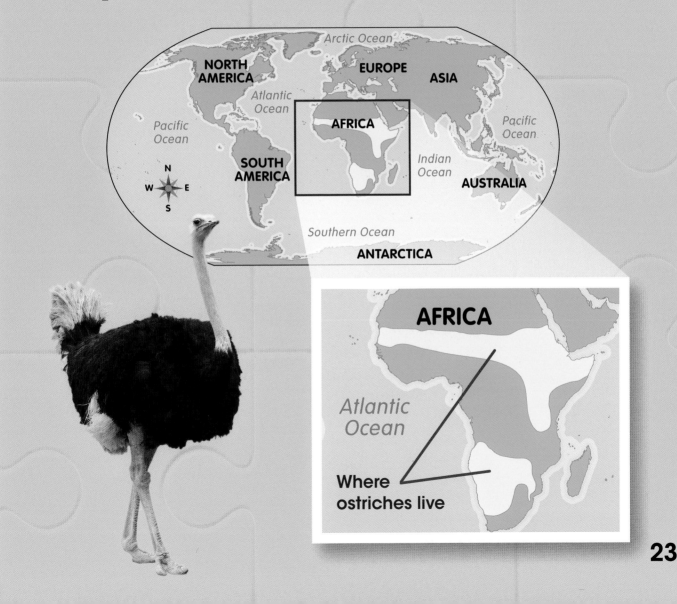

Where ostriches live

23

Index

Read More

Ripple, William John. *Ostriches (Desert Animals).* Mankato, MN: Capstone (2005).

Spilsbury, Louise. *Ostrich (A Day in the Life: Grassland Animals).* Chicago: Heinemann (2011).

Learn More Online

To learn more about ostriches, visit
www.bearportpublishing.com/ZooClues

About the Author

Joyce Markovics lives along the Hudson River in Tarrytown, New York. She enjoys spending time with furry, finned, and feathered creatures.